Chuck Swindoll

For Those Who Hurt

MULTNOMAH PRESS
Portland, Oregon 97266

Photography by David Cavagnaro,
Gerry Mettler
Design by Dannelle L. Pfeiffer

Printed in Singapore

Library of Congress Card Number: 77-4594
ISBN 0-930014-13-8

88 89 90 – 15 14 13

About Chuck Swindoll:

John R. W. Stott says that it's very easy to be faithful if you do not care about being contemporary, and it's also easy to be contemporary if you do not bother to be faithful. Few men of God on the scene today can strike that delicate balance. As a pastor to a large, growing congregation, as a radio speaker, as an author and as a husband and father, Chuck Swindoll has achieved that rare equilibrium . . . a contemporary, faithful communicator of God's Word.

Chuck Swindoll is also the author of:

Anger
Come Before Winter
Committment
Demonism
Destiny
Divorce
Encourage Me
Eternal Security
Growing Strong in the
    Seasons of Life
Hope
Integrity
Killing Giants, Pulling
    Thorns

Leisure
Moral Purity
Our Mediator
Sensuality
Singleness
Standing Out
Starting Over
Stress
Strike the Original Match
Tongues
When Your Comfort Zone
    Gets the Squeeze
Woman

*"What a wonderful God we have—He is the Father of
our Lord Jesus Christ, the source of every mercy, and
the one who so wonderfully comforts and strengthens us
in our hardships and trials. And why does He do this?
So that when others are troubled, needing our sympathy
and encouragement, we can pass on to them this same
help and comfort God has given us. You can be sure that
the more we undergo sufferings for Christ, the more He
will shower us with His comfort and encouragement.
We are in deep trouble for bringing you God's comfort
and salvation. But in our trouble God has comforted
us—and this, too, to help you: to show you from our
personal experience how God will tenderly comfort you
when you undergo these same sufferings. He will give
you the strength to endure.*

*I think you ought to know, dear brothers, about the
hard time we went through in Asia. We were really
crushed and overwhelmed, and feared we would never
live through it. We felt we were doomed to die and saw
how powerless we were to help ourselves; but that was
good, for then we put everything into the hands of God,
who alone could save us, for He can even raise the
dead. And He did help us, and saved us from a terrible
death; yes, and we expect Him to do it again and
again. But you must help us too, by praying for us. For
much thanks and praise will go to God from you who
see His wonderful answers to your prayers for our
safety!"*

(2 Corinthians 1:3-11, Living Bible).

FOR
those
who
hurt

Why Me? Why Now? Why This?

El Tablazo looked so close. Too close. It happened so fast. Exploding into the jagged 14,000 foot peak, the DC-4 disintegrated with a metallic scream.

What was left of the Avianca Airline flight bound for Quito, Ecuador, flamed crazily down the mountainside into a deep ravine. One awful moment illuminated a cold Colombian mountain in the night, then the darkness returned. And the silence.

Before leaving the airport, earlier that day, a young New Yorker named Glenn Chambers hurriedly scribbled a note on a piece of paper he found on the floor of the terminal. The scrap was part of a printed advertisement with the single word "WHY" sprawled across the center.

Needing stationery in a hurry, Chambers scrawled a note to his mother around the word in the middle. Quickly folding this last-minute thought, he stuffed it in an envelope and dropped it in a box. There would be more to come, of course. More about the budding of a lifelong dream to begin a ministry with the Voice of the Andes in Ecuador.

But there was no more to come. Between the mailing and the delivery of Chambers' note, El Tablazo snagged his flight and his dreams from the night sky. The envelope arrived later than the news of his death. When his mother received it, the question burned up at her from the page— WHY?

It is the question that hits first and lingers longest. Why? Why me? Why now? Why this? Maybe you feel like the woman who wrote:

> *Lord, I'm drowning*
> *In a sea of perplexity.*
> *Waves of confusion*
> *Crash over me.*
> *I'm too weak*
> *To shout for help.*
> *Either quiet the waves*
> *Or lift me above them—*
> *It's too late*
> *To learn to swim.*

The following words will not answer all your whys. There is only One who can do that. All of the insights on the next few pages are designed to have you look up into the face of God. He knows you are hurting and is ready to help.

Getting Ready

We cannot prepare for a crisis *after* that crisis occurs. Preparation must take place *before* we are nose to nose with the issue.

Sometimes we are barely keeping balance on the spiritual tightrope as we are ... then something shakes the rope! Disaster blows in the door.

Proverbs 24:10 refers to this:

"If you are slack in the day of distress, your strength is limited."

If the "day of distress" caused you to stagger and slump into depression, your strength was small. In other words, the real test of your spiritual stability does not come while your little pond is free from ripples. It comes when the waves of suffering roll in. If you maintain an optimistic, faithful outlook, your strength is great. You were properly prepared for the day of distress.

Consider Jeremiah 12:5:

"If you have run with footmen and they have tired you out, then how can you compete with horses? If you fall down in a land of peace, how will you do in the thicket of the Jordan?"

If you are limping along, barely able to handle life's pressures when things are fairly peaceful—stumbling along with the infantry—what are you going to do when the cavalry charges into the scene? What are you going to do when jungle warfare erupts, when you have to double-time through the thicket?

God wants you to be properly prepared for the days of affliction. He wants to clothe you for the thorns of the thicket.

God Is Involved

Like a series of devastating dominoes, Job lost his crops, his cattle, his home, his prosperity, his children and finally, his health. On top of all this, his unsympathetic wife advised him to "curse God and die."

Bankrupt and broken, he spent many days listening to a few so-called counselors who pointed self-righteous fingers and blamed him for all of his own trouble.

On one occasion, he replied to the accusations with words of amazing wisdom:

> "He knows the way I take; when He has tried me, I shall come forth as gold. My foot has held fast to His path; I have kept His way and not turned aside. I have not departed from the command of His lips; I have treasured the words of His mouth more than my necessary food. But He is unique and who can turn Him? And what His soul desires, that He does" (Job 23:10-13).

Do you hear what he's saying?

"God desired to bring these troubles into my life. He knows what is best. I refuse to turn aside in doubt."

This man who knew the flash-flood of sudden trouble as well as the long, long days of persisting pain, said:

> *"He performs what is appointed for me"*
> *(Job 23:14)*.

God performs—brings about—causes—what is *appointed for me.* This suffering that I face—*all suffering*—is exactly as God designed it. You will never learn the lessons God wants to teach you until you realize this.

Your trouble is God—ordained. He either appoints the affliction, or allows it to happen *for your good.*

The Bible erases all doubt concerning this:

> *"And we know that God causes all things to work together for good to those who love God, to those who are called according to His purpose"*
> *(Romans 8:28)*.

Let's confirm two facts we've discovered in Scripture:

Fact one: We should be prepared for suffering *before* the suffering occurs.

Fact two: Whatever the affliction, it has been appointed or approved by God, our heavenly Father, *for our good*.

If these twin truths are cemented in your mind, you are ready for the first chapter of 2 Corinthians.

This is a personal letter. It wasn't easy for Paul to write. Pulling back the curtain, the Apostle bares his deep personal struggle and allows us to glimpse something of what he had to endure.

Years ago, I took a red marking pencil and circled all the terms in this letter pertaining to suffering, such as "affliction," "distress" and "troubles." By the time I finished, there were red marks *throughout* the book.

Second Corinthians is also God's personal letter, written by Him and addressed to you. You who are hurting. Closer than anything else, this book approaches the "Why" question.

A deeper look at the first chapter reveals three important reasons for suffering.

Why Do We Suffer?

There may be dozens of reasons why we suffer, but Paul highlights three. With your Bible open to 2 Corinthians 1:1-11, take a pencil and circle the little four-letter word "that" in verses 4, 9, and 11. Each of the three reasons is introduced with "that."

Let's begin by looking at verses 1 through 4.

"Paul, an apostle of Christ Jesus by the will of God, and Timothy our brother, to the church of God which is at Corinth with all the saints who are throughout Achaia: Grace to you and peace from God our Father and the Lord Jesus Christ. Blessed be the God and Father of our Lord Jesus Christ, the Father of mercies and God of all comfort; who comforts us in all our affliction so that we may be able to comfort those who are in any affliction with the comfort with which we ourselves are comforted by God."

If you were to read down through verse 7, your attention would be called to a term that appears no less than ten times—"comfort." this is from the Greek terms PARA, meaning "beside, alongside," and KALEO, "to call." *Called alongside.*

This is no shallow sympathy card with rhyming words and gold-glitter greeting. It is eternally more than a "slap on the back" or a quick "cheer up" bit of advice. Our mighty God is *called alongside* as we suffer! Here is genuine comfort, personal assistance, deep involvement and infinite understanding.

Notice that God admits He is the *God of all comfort*. Regardless of the need, God comforts. No matter the cause, God gets personally involved in your life, suffering friend. He is the God of *all* comfort! That's His specialty.

Then observe that He comforts those who are *in any affliction*. That draws the circle around your situation. Any and every affliction is His concern.

> "*For we do not have a high priest who cannot sympathize with our weaknesses, but one who has been tempted in all things as we are, yet without sin*" (Heb. 4:15).

> "*Casting all your anxiety upon Him, because He cares for you*" (1 Peter 5:7).

He genuinely cares—deeply cares. But why are we afflicted?

That We Might Be Prepared To Comfort Others

Who can understand what it is like to sit along-side a friend or loved one dying with a terminal

illness? Who knows the heartache of having a home split apart? What about someone to understand the loss of a child...or the misery of a teen-ager on drugs...or the anguish of living with an alcoholic mate...or a failure in school...or the loss of a business? Who on earth understands?

I'll tell you who—the person who has been through it wrapped in the blanket of God's comfort. Better than anybody else. You who have endured the stinging experiences are the choicest counselors God can use.

This is one of the reasons we suffer—to be prepared to bring encouragement and comfort to others who come across our path enduring a similar situation. Remember that!

Look back at the chain reaction. We suffer... God comes alongside to comfort...others suffer ...we step alongside to comfort them. With God's arm firmly around my shoulders, I have the strength and stability to place my arm around the shoulder of another. Isn't this true? Similar experiences create mutual understanding.

Because of this we can confidently say that our troubling circumstances are *never* in vain. The bruises may hurt, but they are not without reason. God is uniquely preparing us for the comfort others will need. In one sense, we are all "preparing for the ministry." Our Father is preparing us to meet the deep inner needs of others by bringing us through the dark places first.

Notice verses 8–10.

"For we do not want you to be unaware, brethren, of our affliction which came to us in Asia, that we were burdened excessively, beyond our strength, so that we despaired even of life; indeed we had the sentence of death within ourselves in order that we should not trust in ourselves, but in God who raises the dead; who delivered us from so great a peril of death, and will deliver us, He on whom we have set our hope. And He will yet deliver us."

We wish we knew more about Paul's experience in Asia. All we know is that the battered apostle was pushed to the very edge of his endurance. And then a little bit farther. No walls left to lean on, no water left in the well, no fine phrases left to repeat in the face of crisis—the face of death. Paul said, "This is it. End of the rope, end of the line."

Perhaps these words are your words. Maybe you are standing with Paul at the desperate point beyond your own strength. Hope has quietly slipped out the back door. The despair is beyond repair. Burdens push heavy on bruised inner tissue. The end has come!

Unbelievable as it may seem, God has a reason even in this.

That We Might
Not Trust
In Ourselves

Did you miss this truth, wedged in verse nine?
Paul puts his finger on another reason for our
season of sorrow: that we might come to a complete
end of ourselves and learn the power of total dependence.

When Paul's own strength had ebbed away, he
found another strength. When his own will to go
on faded like the last morning star, the sun of a new
hope blazed on his horizon.

When he finally hit bottom, Paul learned that he
was in the palm of God's hand. He could sink no
lower than the Everlasting Arms.

Let me remind you of God's dealings with His
friend, Abraham, in Genesis 22. The very first
verse of that chapter tells us that *God tested Abraham*. In fact, He told Abraham to take his
beloved son Isaac to a mountain called Moriah and

offer him up as a burnt offering. Though the old man's heart hemorrhaged within him, he did not argue—he obeyed. What a test! Clinging only to his hope in God, Abraham cooperated.

On that stark mountain a few days later, the aged patriarch raised a sharpened knife—poised to plunge into the heart of the son he loved. (Think of it!) But God stepped in and stayed his hand.

You ask, "How could Abraham actually carry out such a plan in an obedient manner?" The answer is tucked away in Hebrews 11:17-19, which says:

> "By faith Abraham, when he was tested, offered up Isaac; and he who had received the promises was offering up his only begotten son: it was he to whom it was said, IN ISAAC YOUR DESCENDENTS SHALL BE CALLED. He considered that God is able to raise men even from the dead …"

Abraham was determined to shift the weight of his trust from himself to God, who "is able to raise men even from the dead." And this, the Bible calls "faith."

Perhaps I am writing to a stubborn, suffering saint who is wrestling with God over an affliction. You have not yet laid down your arms and decided to trust in Him completely.

Can't you see, my friend, that God is trying to teach you the all-important lesson of submission to Him—total dependence on His infinite wisdom and unbounded love? He will not let up until you give up, believe me. Who knows better than God that case-hardened independence within you? How much longer are you going to fight God? In Psalm 46:10, He says to us:

"Cease striving and know that I am God ..."

Cease striving—be still!
Surrender to your Lord...*now*. He does not design your ruin—only your refinement.

" 'For I know the plans that I have for you,' declares the Lord, 'plans for welfare and not for calamity to give you a future and a hope' " (Jeremiah 29:11).

The great hymn, HOW FIRM A FOUNDATION says it best:

When through fiery trials
thy pathway shall lie,
My grace all-sufficient
shall be thy supply

The flame shall not hurt thee,
I only design
Thy dross to consume
And thy gold to refine.

Years ago, I came across a statement which has returned to my thoughts again and again:

Pain plants the flag of reality
In the fortress of a rebel heart.

Pain reduces us to a primary level, the level of dependence on our God. While we stretch out full length on Him, everything within us that is useless and abrasive is simply melted away. Those who were hard and harsh are humbled in Him. Those once proud and self-sufficient are drawn to their knees.

Suffering reveals our creature status. We are not all-wise or infinite in strength. But God is. And we need Him—*we were created to need Him.* Desperately. Sometimes it takes coming to the end of ourselves to see that. God knows. We need to take everything we were, everything we are and everything we've ever hoped to be and simply place it all in the nail-scarred hands of our loving Lord. And lean hard upon His Word.

Andráe Crouch, a contemporary composer, captures this truth in a song called:

THROUGH IT ALL

I've had many tears and sorrow,
I've had questions for tomorrow;
There've been times I didn't know right from
    wrong
But in ev'ry situation, God gave blessed
    consolation
That my trials come to only make me
    strong.

I've been to lots of places,
And I've seen a lot of faces;
There've been times I felt so all alone,
But in my lonely hours,
Yes, those precious, lonely hours
Jesus let me know that I was His Own.

I thank God for the mountains and I thank
    Him for the valleys,
I thank Him for the storms He brought me
    through,
For if I'd never had a problem
I wouldn't know that He could solve them,
I'd never know what faith in God could do.

Through it all, through it all,
Oh, I've learned to trust in Jesus,
I've learned to trust in God.
Through it all, through it all,
I've learned to depend upon His Word.

That We Might Learn To Give Thanks In Everything

Y ou'll never be able to understand this third reason, until you've grappled with the first two.

Notice how Paul phrases this to his Corinthian friends in verse 11.

"...*You also joining in helping us through your prayers, that thanks may be given by many persons on our behalf for the favor bestowed upon us through the prayers of many.*"

He wrote them a thank-you note. Looking upon his suffering as an opportunity to share his life with others, Paul felt drawn to the Corinthians with cords tied to the innermost being. As they mutually joined in and helped him through their prayers, thanks was rendered to God by many persons.

Because of Paul's encounter with affliction, many were led to focus on the Lord Jesus Christ and give thanks. One man offered praise in his moment of sorrow, and God so multiplied his song it became a great chorus, echoing in antiphonal voice from heart after heart.

God is interested in using us as *living* object lessons to others. That is precisely why He urges us to present ourselves as *living* sacrifices. What might happen in your life if you stopped fighting God and started to praise Him for your pain?

Try telling Him that you want to be *His* living object lesson of patience and stability to others. Tell Him how grateful you are for the crushing blows He has chosen to bring into your life.

In your own way and in your own words, express how very thankful you are that He has selected you from the ranks of millions to share in "the fellowship of His sufferings," and, like Christ, to "learn obedience from the things which you suffer." You will be a rare, refined believer if you respond to suffering in this manner, child of God.

Job responded in a similar manner when he said:

"Why should I take my flesh in my teeth, and put my life in my hands? Though He slay me, I will hope in Him" (Job 13:14-15).

If Job could lift his face and say that to God, so can you. "Lord—even though this is the most difficult experience of my life, my hope is in You. Thank You for this canyon of pain. I'm leaning on You as I go through it."

A whole new dimension is opened up to the one who learns to give God thanks for His plan... pain notwithstanding.

Looking Back

God allows our suffering:

That we might be prepared to comfort others.
That we might not trust in ourselves.
That we might learn to give thanks in
*   everything.*

Don't doubt for a moment that circumstances of suffering are used of God to shape you and conform you into the "image of His Son ..." *Nothing* enters your life accidentally—remember that. There is no such thing as "luck" or "coincidence" or "blind faith" to the child of God. Behind our every experience is our loving, sovereign Lord. He is continually working things out according to His infinite plan and purpose. And that includes our suffering.

When God wants to do an impossible task, He takes an impossible individual...and crushes him. Being crushed means being reshaped—to be a vital, useful instrument in His hands.

Some Thoughts On Tears

When words fail, tears flow.

Tears have a language all their own, a tongue that needs no interpreter. In some mysterious way, our complex inner-communication system knows when to admit its verbal limitations...and the tears come.

Eyes that flashed and sparkled only moments before are flooded from a secret reservoir. We try in vain to restrain the flow, but even strong men falter.

Tears are not self-conscious. They can spring upon us when we are speaking in public, or standing beside others who look to us for strength. Most often they appear when our soul is overwhelmed with feelings that words cannot describe.

Our tears may flow during the singing of a great, majestic hymn, or when we are alone, lost in some vivid memory or wrestling in prayer.

Did you know that God takes special notice of those tears of yours? Psalm 56:8 tells us that He puts them in His bottle and enters them into the record He keeps on our lives.

David said, "The Lord has heard the voice of my weeping."

A teardrop on earth summons the King of Heaven. Rather than being ashamed or disappointed, the Lord takes note of our inner friction when hard times are oiled by tears. He turns these situations into moments of tenderness; He never forgets those crises in our lives where tears were shed.

One of the great drawbacks of our cold, sophisticated society is its reluctance to showing tears. For some strange reason, men feel that tears are a sign of weakness...and many an adult feels it's immature. How silly! How unfortunate! The consequence is that we place a watchdog named "restraint" before our hearts. This animal is trained to bark, snap and scare away any unexpected guest who seeks entrance.

The ultimate result is a well-guarded, highly respectable, uninvolved heart surrounded by heavy bars of confinement. Such a structure resembles a prison more than a home where the tender Spirit of Christ resides.

Jeremiah lived in no such dwelling. His transparent tent was so tender and sensitive he could not preach a sermon without the interruption of tears. "The weeping prophet" became his nickname and even though he didn't always have the words to describe his feelings, he was never at a loss to communicate his convictions. You could always count on Jeremiah to bury his head in his hands and sob aloud.

Strange that this man was selected by God to be His personal spokesman at the most critical time in Israel's history. Seems like an unlikely choice—unless you value tears as God does. I wonder how many tear bottles in heaven are marked with his name.

I wonder how many of them bear *your* initials. You'll never have many until you impound restraint and let a little tenderness run loose. You might lose a little of your polished respectability, but you'll have a lot more freedom. And a lot less pride.

Looking Ahead

So... here you are facing an uncertain future. You can be fearful and fretful... or calm and quiet. You can worry, or rest... struggle or surrender.

While in severe pain, a man of God named Horatius Bonar recorded his response in verse, calling it:

CHOOSE THOU FOR ME:

Thy way, not mine, O Lord,
However dark it be!
Lead me by Thine own hand;
Choose out my path for me.
I dare not choose my lot:
I would not, if I might;
Choose Thou for me, my God,
So shall I walk aright....

The kingdom that I seek
Is Thine: so let the way
That leads to it be Thine,
Else I must surely stray.
Take Thou my cup, and it
With joy or sorrow fill,
As best to Thee may seem;
Choose Thou my good and ill.

Choose Thou for me my friends,
My sickness, or my health;
Choose Thou my cares for me
My poverty, or wealth.
Not mine, not mine the choice,
In things both great and small;
Be Thou my Guide, my Strength,
My Wisdom, and my all.

Could it be that God seems distant to you right now? Perhaps He does not seem to be your Guide, your Strength, your Wisdom and your all. If this is true, then my words have offered little comfort or hope. Just empty words arranged around some colorful pictures. Nothing more.

You may feel He is far away but the truth is, He is near... more real than the pain you are enduring. He longs to support you in the crucible of crisis. Trust Him today. Like a child, look up into the Father's face. His arms are open, not closed. His Son, Jesus Christ, is ready to enter your life if you will only invite Him to do so. Right now.

He will hear you.

He has a special love ... for those who hurt.